CAT TALES

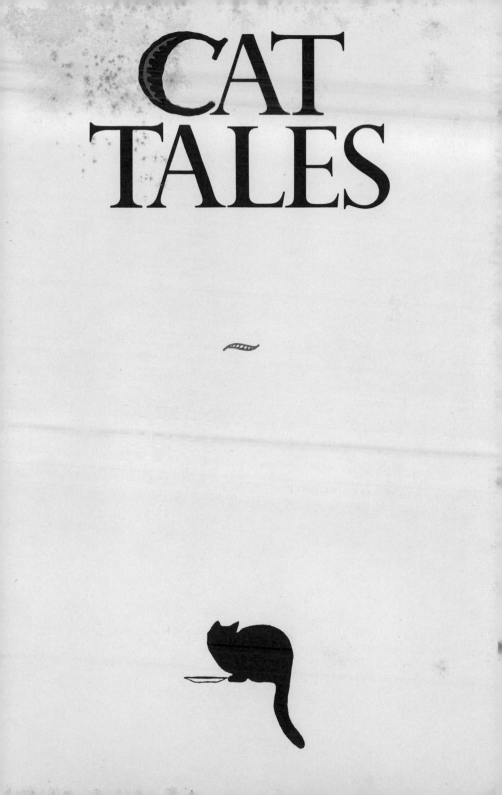

CAT

TALES

FOLK TALES
COLLECTED AND
RETOLD

BY MALACHI
McCORMICK

CLARKSON N. POTTER, INC./PUBLISHERS
NEW YORK

FOR
PEARLIE
AND
PEANUTS

I would like to express my appreciation to the unnamed chroniclers of folk tales down through the ages. About half of these tales were originally published by me in a handmade edition. Some wonderful people at Clarkson N. Potter assisted in the transition: Carolyn Hart, Amy Schuler, and Jan Melchior; and my good friend and agent, Susan Bergholz. Also, Pearlie and Peanuts, who posed as cats for the duration.

Grateful acknowledgment is made for permission to reprint the following
copyrighted material:

Excerpt from "Mehitabel has an adventure" by Don Marquis,
reprinted by permission of Doubleday, a division of Bantam, Doubleday,
Dell Publishing Group, Inc.

Excerpt from "Prothalamion" by W. H. Auden in *The English Auden*, edited by
Edward Mendelson, copyright © 1976 by Edward Mendelson, William Meredith,
and Monroe K. Spears, executors of the estate of W. H. Auden. Reprinted by
permission of Random House, Inc.

Published by Clarkson N. Potter, Inc., and distributed by Crown Publishers, Inc.,
201 East 50th Street, New York, New York 10022

CLARKSON N. POTTER, POTTER, and colophon are trademarks of Clarkson N.
Potter, Inc.

Manufactured in the United States of America

Design by Jan Melchior

Library of Congress Cataloging-in-Publication Data
McCormick, Malachi.
Cat tales: folk tales/collected and retold by Malachi McCormick
p.   cm.
1. Cats—Folklore.   I. Title.
GR725.M39   1989
398.2′452974428—dc19   89–3817

ISBN 0-517-57256-7
1   3   5   7   9   10   8   6   4   2

First Edition

CONTENTS

INTRODUCTION

We Cat Folk will readily acknowledge that our Beloved Puss, for all her intimate ubiquity, remains to us a mysterious puzzlement.

Of course we delight in her wit, her intelligence, and her liquid agility. Her curiosity and her cleanliness are clichés, but no less remarkable for that. We envy her her natural sense of diplomacy and her unself-conscious style.

Her extraordinary evolution is a source of endless wonderment. How *did* a tiger become a cat? I wondered for years, never suspecting that it might be the opposite, which apparently is the case: The evolving cat became a tiger, giving us yet another reason to be nice to her!!

We Cat Lovers will readily admit that there is hardly one of Dear Puss's attributes that we would not wish to have more of for ourselves. (However, I would tend to advocate trying self-improvement and New Year's resolutions first before going around the corner to your local gene-splicer.)

While we are talking frankly, let us admit that "Cat Lover" hardly serves: "Lover" implies equality. No, we are Cat Servants, are we not, happy in our work, with a master the hem of whose garment is in unending need of touching. And not just the hem—the whole furry garment!

Theophile Gautier had it right: "God made the cat that we might have the pleasure of embracing the tiger."

It is quite apparent from this collection of cat folk tales that our pleasure in embracing our domestic tiger is shared

across the available geography, and through most of history.

There is much here for our amusement and delight.

But Dear Puss has also suffered much, at different times in her history, because of the ignorance and the fears of humans, and this is reflected in some of the stories. What an account she could give us of her own history, and what she could tell us about ourselves would not be all flattering.

While researching these stories, it became apparent to me that there are many more folk tales devoted to cats than to any other animal. There is an obvious reason for this: Puss's mysterious inscrutability, despite her universal in-house presence. Indeed, her fabled independence and aloofness have served only to increase our speculation about her, all in the lamentable absence of catspeak.

A good story, it is said, tells us about its subject, while a bad story reveals more about its author. And there are both here, in the human perceptions and projections that make up these folk tales. We delight in the many wonderful faces of the Composite Cat. Some, however, inform us more of the imperfections of humans than the perfection of Puss.

Think of it: Unique among all the animals, she has been regarded by us as both Deity and Devil. She has been loved and feared; revered and reviled; worshipped and persecuted.

The ancient Egyptians seem to have been the first to coax the cat down from the hills and out of the wilderness, and into their houses. There are depictions of cats dating from about 2600 B.C., although the degree of domesticity is not clear until later. One tomb-painting shows Puss observing the action from under her master's chair. Another shows a cat with a red ribbon leash which is tied to her master's stool.

In ancient Egypt the cat—symbol of the Goddess Bast (or Pasht, from which name, apparently, the affectionate-familiar "Puss" derives)—was widely worshipped. Bast was a benevolent Goddess in Egypt's pantheon, overseeing such matters as fecundity and beauty, and was immensely popular.

Diodorus, a contemporary historian, tells of an event that shows us how the Egyptians felt about their cats: "When one of these [sacred] animals is concerned, he who kills one . . . is put to death. The populace flings itself on him, and cruelly maltreats him, usually before he can be tried and judged. In the days when . . . the people of Egypt still hastened to welcome all visitors from Italy, . . . and carefully avoided any occasion for complaint, . . . a Roman killed a cat. The populace crowded to the house of the Roman . . . and neither the efforts of magistrates . . . nor the fear of Rome could avail to save the man's life, though what he had done was admitted to be accidental. This is not . . . from hearsay, but something I saw myself during my sojourn in Egypt."

In fact, however, the deliberate killing of a cat was a capital offence in those days in Egypt.

Herodotus, the wonderful source of so much of our knowledge of ancient Egypt, cites a multitude of "cat" practices that make enthralling reading. He tells us, for instance, that upon the death of their cat, an entire family would shave off their eyebrows and for several hours loudly lament poor Puss's passing. The mummified body of the cat would be placed in a sarcophagus. The wealthier the family, the more elaborate would be the funeral. One cat tomb, excavated in the late 1800s, contained the mummies of some twenty cats, with little pots nearby which had contained offerings of milk.

The worship and proper care of the household cat was meticulously handed down from father to son. Sacred cats watched over the temples, where Bast's priests scrutinized and interpreted their every stretch, purr, and meow.

Herodotus relates an instance in which a building catches fire, but the family's first concern is to rescue its cat, "whose death to them seemed more painful than any other loss."

He also tells us of the practice of embalming cats, and indeed great multitudes of mummified cats have been found, with little mouse-mummies laid out beside them. A symbol of an age-old conflict finally resolved? Or, put there for Puss's eternal diversion, a sort of feline viaticum? Herodotus, who gives so many answers, this time leaves us hanging.

Of course there were also some very practical reasons to hold the cat in such high and loving regard. After all, it was Puss who saved the Egyptian granaries, upon which Egypt's glorious civilization was built, from the ravaging hordes of rats and mice.

Many other cultures also held the cat in high esteem, and had laws specifically protecting cats. In 10th-century Celtic Wales, for instance, a person would be compensated for the loss of an adult cat with sixty bushels of grain. Tokyo, to this day, has the famous Go-To-Ku-Ji cat cemetery, in the middle of which is a temple which is served by priests who wear sacred robes and who chant for the repose of cat souls. There are numerous other extraordinary examples.

But in Europe, trouble was on the way. As the Catholic church expanded its influence there, it waged a fierce war for the hearts, minds, and souls of the people, against the earlier religions, all of which it tarred with the same brush.

To the Church in the Middle Ages, cats were inextricably bound up with paganism, witchcraft, and devil-worship: They had to be dealt with. Since the coercive sacrament of forced baptism would presumably be wasted on a cat, a Cat Inquisition was begun that would have made Torquemada proud. The long and arduous business of exterminating Europe's cats was undertaken, with burnings, drownings and impalings, and all those other tricks of the inquisitor's trade.

To say the least, the Church's timing in all of this was unfortunate. It had barely completed its bloody work in time for the Black Death to arrive, the rat-borne plague that killed off seventy-five million people in the four years from 1347 to 1351. The rats, who ironically had first been imported into Europe on the ships of returning Crusaders, were able to go about spreading the Black Death at their leisure, unchecked.

What a dreadful reign of terror—and with what disastrous repercussions!

By contrast, we are happy for Puss's sake that she seems to have been treated better in most other parts of the world.

It has been sardonically remarked that cats apparently refrain from engaging in witchcraft where people do not believe in witches. It is also interesting to note that the more emotionally healthy tales in this collection come from what we like to call the third world.

What is it about cats that brings out the ailurophobe in religions? We have already dealt with the dismal Catholic record (despite that ironic suggestion of "Cat-a-holic"!). The Protestants, with that famous work ethic, immediately rolled up their sleeves and made up for their late arrival on the scene with an equal cruelty. Under their aegis, a later phase of the cat witch hunt spread to America. As will be seen

here, Judaism has a legend that claims that God created neither cat nor pig, probably because (I speculate) their ancient Middle East neighbors, the Egyptians, venerated the cat, and the Chaldeans the pig. (One wonders if the reason that the Plagues of Egypt did not include a glaringly obvious "Plague of Rats" was that Yahweh knew that the Egyptians had the perfect answer to such a plague.)

The Muslims have an almost identical story in which God does not create the cat. And oddly, Buddhism, the religion of compassion, exhibits similar anti-cat prejudices. Such prejudices, it seems, have more lives than do cats, and die hard. In these fundamentalism-prone times we encounter the occasional resonance: We hear it pointed out that, funny, the cat is not mentioned in the Bible! To which there is only one reply, equally logical: Neither is Velcro or Jimmy Swaggart!

I have often wondered about this deep-seated hostility toward cats: Where does it come from?

I got a clue from friends who are allergic to cats: A small percentage of the population is, and presumably always has been, allergic to cats. Some reactions cause mild discomfort. Others are more severe, and these sufferers feel that it is physical torture to enter a cat environment.

But there is another category beyond this one. Some sufferers, when they come into the presence of a cat, feel quite literally in imminent danger of being suffocated to death!

Today we know how allergies work. But what explanation, short of diabolical possession, would such people have given in the Middle Ages? Might they not conclude: "Cats are evil. They hold a diabolical power of life and death over people, and use it silently and capriciously, out of sheer malevolence. Cats must be put down!" And so they did their best.

But, dear reader, do not despair! There have been great improvements, and great champions of the cat along the way, from the 13th-century sultan of Cairo who bequeathed to the neighborhood cats the revenue from his orchard, a bequest that continued into the 19th century; to Cardinal Richelieu, who left a large sum of money for the continued well-being of his cats. This concern has endured right down to Marjorie Horton, who in 1989, wrote a Putnam Valley library out of her will for dismissing Muffin, the library cat of seven years standing, because a trustee was allergic and because there were allegations that Muffin had also "swatted some children without provocation." Hah! Without provocation? What were those kids doing in the library, anyway? Shouldn't they have been in a video arcade?

And there is further encouragement. A recent report in the *New York Times* put the total number of cat pets in the United States at over fifty-six million! That, as someone rightly observed, is a lot of cats! Though the report did not mention the equivalent dog demographics, it made clear that Puss has outstripped Prince and become our most popular pet!

It is a statistic as ironic as it is hopeful for all parties, when one considers that the animal that has suffered most at our hands has ended up in our laps. And purring too.

All's well that ends well!

THE CAT IN INCHIGEELA GRAVEYARD

Irish

This folktale from Ireland is a particular favorite of mine. In the first place, Macroom and Inchigeela, in West Cork, are very familiar places to me, because we had relatives there. A Fair Day in the town square at Macroom made a fierce and fascinating impression on a young lad, with its cracked choreography of cagey farmers and shrilly complaining animals. For sheer urgency, it's hard to beat the near-seizured squealing pig or, for outrage, the affronted rooster looking for respect. I remember the way the farmers made their deals, the insulted rejection of the first offer, which was always "pathetic;" the pantomime of disinterest; and then the vigorous spitting on the palms to close the deal. I remember the rumbustious traffic in the pubs in the square; Brueghel and Hogarth both would have felt very much at home. I remember the endless music, with a soaring brassy trumpet from the dance band at the Town Hall late that night, which kept me awake. The images are conjured up in a twinkling.

But there's another aspect to this story that appeals to me: It represents a particularly Irish "side" to the cat, to wit, the Mysterious Animal, with mysterious powers—a being deserving of

our admiration, demanding our respect, one not to be trifled with.

And—just to clear something up—it is not in the least surprising that a cat should stick its head through the railings of a graveyard and speak to a farmer, and on equal terms too, mind you. Indeed, it was an event so commonplace as to have slipped the farmer's mind completely!

It's a long time ago now that it happened, on the day of the Macroom Fair. In those days it took a long time to go a short distance, and you'd be traveling in your horse and trap half the night to get there in time for the start of the fair.

This one particular night there was a fierce pelting rain and by the time we got to Macroom I was as wet as a drownded rat.

The day wasn't much better. I had only a few hens to sell, and there was a great scarcity of money. By the end of the fair, I had hardly enough for a packet of tea for herself and a twist of tobacco for me.

Anyway, I took a drink at the end of the day, and soon the horse and myself were back on the road to Ballingeary. With the wretched old rain still coming down we had only one thought in our two heads: to get home, have a spot of grub—and then hit the hay, be it bed or stable!

Well, a queer thing happened when we got to Inchigeela. To tell you the truth, I was as good as asleep by then, but as we passed the graveyard, a big black tom cat sticks his head through a stile, cocks it to one side, and says to me: "Tell Balgurry that Balgarry is dead!"

It was midnight easy by the time we finally got home, and

I was about ready to collapse, but herself had me supper ready, and a good cup of tea, and of course, anxious to hear all the news.

"Well," says she, "How was it?"

"Yerra, only fair to middling."

"And who did ye see?"

"Yerra, nobody much."

"What did the hens fetch?"

"Ah, there was no money about at all, at all."

"Was there any news of Seamus?"

"Divil a bit!"

She's exasperated with me: "Aren't you the fine one to send out for news. Have you nothing at all to say for yourself?"

I puff my pipe and take a swig of tea: "Well, there was one queer thing that happened today. Just as I was going by the graveyard at Inchigeela, what do I see but a black tom cat in the stile, and him talking to me!"

"And what did he say?"

"He said, 'Tell Balgurry that Balgarry is dead!' "

Well, at the mention of this, up jumps our own cat, who had been asleep by the fire. He berates me: "The Divil take you. What took ye so long to deliver the message? Now I'll be late for the funeral!"

And—would you credit it—she takes off up the chimney in a mad bolt, and we never laid eyes on her again, from that day to this.

THE ORIGINAL PUSS-IN-BOOTS

Italian

"A CAT MAY LOOK AT A KING."—PROVERB

Puss-in-Boots *is my nomination for folklore's most lovable rogue. Puss is a real operator, a confidence cat, who has a field day with human vanities and frailties. He can talk his way into anything—and out again! If he showed up today, it would surely be as a junk bond wizard on Wall Street!*

And he exploits us readers almost as much as his victims in the story, working on that ambivalence we seem to feel toward the confidence trickster: His deceit infringes the law, but we wink at it because he follows a higher law (facilitating that old Darwinian process) by exploiting those characteristics that we feel deserve to be exploited, namely greed and gullibility. (As long as it's not our own greed and gullibility. Excuse me, I should say astuteness and trust.) I remember being enthralled by the wonderful and elaborate (and true) story of the man who sold the "eyesore" of the Eiffel Tower to an overeager scrap-metal merchant.

Puss would know where to get you a tower cheap. And maybe even throw in a suspension bridge.

A Neapolitan beggar was so poor that when he died he had only a cat to leave to his son. The son, named

Gagliuso, was bemoaning his misfortune, but Puss said to him: "Oh for heavens sake stop whining! I could make you rich, if I put my mind to it." The son was depressed and dismissed the idea.

But Puss had a plan. Every day, he went off to catch a fish, which he took to the king, saying: "My Lord Gagliuso, your Majesty's most humble servant, craves your indulgence, and with respect, sends you this fish."

Passing the kitchen one day, Puss overheard the chief cook complain that there were no gamebirds for the king's dinner. Whereupon he went to the poultry market to "borrow" some quail and ortolan, which he obsequiously presented to the king, "from Lord Gagliuso, your most humble servant."

Before long the king felt obliged to thank Lord Gagliuso in person, which presented the problem of what Gagliuso should wear to impress His Majesty. On the morning of the appointed day, Puss came to the palace breathless and in obvious distress: "My Lord Gagliuso's dastardly servants have robbed him overnight, leaving him with not a shirt on his back!" The king duly dispatched some of his own finery, and soon a resplendent Lord Gagliuso was being presented—and banqueted—at court. Puss took the king aside and confided: "My master, Lord Gagliuso, would be most upset with me for telling you this, but he is a man of vast wealth. It occurs to me that perhaps an alliance would benefit you both."

The king sent his valuers to check on the extent of Lord Gagliuso's estates. But crafty Puss went ahead, and wherever he saw sheep, cattle, horses, and so on, he warned their herdsmen: "Beware, a gang of bloodthirsty brigands comes this way. For your own safety, just tell them it all belongs to Lord Gagliuso."

Wherever the king's valuers went, it was the same story! They reported to the king that Puss had, if anything, been modest in describing his master's wealth: *Everything* they saw on the way belonged to Lord Gagliuso!

Now the king took Puss aside and, winking broadly, told him that if Puss could arrange the marriage of his beautiful daughter to Lord Gagliuso, he would certainly make it worth the cat's while. Puss was dubious: "Well, I very much doubt that he will go for it, but I'll see what I can do." Of course, he had no trouble persuading the beggar's son to marry the king's daughter, and accept a fine dowry into the bargain, with which—on the advice of the cat—he bought a huge estate.

(Years later, Gagliuso promised that when Puss died, his body would be preserved in a coffin of gold. To test him, the cat pretended to be dead, and was mortified to hear Gagliuso tell his wife to pick up the dead cat by the tail and chuck it out the window. Whereupon Puss jumped up, berated his ungrateful master, and ran out the door, leaving Gagliuso to look after his own affairs from that day on.)

"Webster was very large and very black and very composed. He conveyed the impression of being a cat of deep reserves. Descendent of a long line of ecclesiastical ancestors who had conducted their decorous courtships beneath the shadow of cathedrals and on the back walls of bishops' palaces, he had that exquisite poise which one sees in the high dignitaries of the Church."

—FROM "THE STORY OF WEBSTER"
BY P. G. WODEHOUSE

HOW THE CAT
CAME TO BE

Jewish

"A GOOD CAT DESERVES A GOOD RAT." — PROVERB

Significantly, neither testament of the Bible makes any reference to cats: My theory is that this is because of what I term the Judeo-Christian Anti-Cat Thing. Consider: You think you want to start a new religion. To your left, those Egyptians are venerating the cat; to your right, the no-good Chaldeans hold the pig to be sacred. What are you going to do? You do the one thing you can do: You make sure those rival "gods" get no respect at all!

Naturally, it was intriguing for me to find this old Jewish legend which makes it amply clear that neither cat nor pig was created by the Great Ineffable One. In fact it is Noah, of Ark fame, who authored both, with what can only be described as a couple of really neat tricks. (Think what he could do with the budget deficit!)

Equally, I find it remarkable that Judaism and Islam share the same, almost identical, legend. The versions appear together here to facilitate comparison.

When the waters of the Great Flood subsided, there were two animals who came off the Ark who had not gone onto it, because they were not created by God.

And this was how this came to pass: After many days, the

people on the Ark came to Noah and entreated him to do something about all the waste that was accumulating. And Noah, who could do many things, went to the Elephant, and quieted it, and passed his hand along the back of the Elephant, and lo, the Pig issued forth, and he devoured all the waste that had accumulated.

A second time the people again came to Noah and protested about the rats that were going about the Ark, eating and destroying the food, and being an annoyance to all who were on the Ark.

And again, Noah, who had many powers, went to the Lion, and quieted him, and then ran his hand down the back of the King of the Beasts. Whereupon the Lion sneezed most violently, and lo, from out of his nostrils sprang a Cat, who immediately ran about devouring the rats.

And from that point the Ark was both clean and free of rats.

"The earliest known members of the modern cat family were smallish animals, about the size of today's African or Asian wild cats. They made their appearance on earth about 13 million years ago. It took about another 10 million years for the big cats—the lions, tigers, leopards—to evolve."

—FROM *THE CAT* BY MURIEL BEADLE

HOW THE CAT
CAME TO BE

Arabic

When Noah brought two of each of the animals onto the Ark, his sons and their wives came to him and said: "What security can there be for us so long as the Lion, King of the Beasts, roameth about this vessel?" And Noah prayed for an answer. And the Lord God sent down a fever from heaven and afflicted the Lion, and tranquility of mind was restored to the sons and their wives. There is no other explanation of the origin of fever in this world.

But there was on the Ark a creature who was also very dangerous, namely the Mouse. And the sons and wives went to Noah and warned him of the danger to them all. And Noah prayed for an answer, and the Most High caused the Lion to sneeze, and the Cat, who had not yet been created, suddenly issued forth from the nose of the King of the Beasts.

And from this time onward, the Mouse turned and became a timid animal, and took up the habit of hiding itself in holes.

THE TRUE NAME
OF THE CAT

Chinese

**"NAMES AND NATURES DO OFTEN
AGREE."—PROVERB**

This elegant and humorous little tale, with its improbable cycle, has a resonance with the plight of the ordinary individual today. Assailed from every quarter with "expert" opinion and advice, he cannot even hope to survive this onslaught without patience, perspicacity, and a healthy dose of common sense. Fortunately, Mr. Chi-Yen possesses all of these qualities in excellent measure.

The naming of a cat is not a task to be taken lightly. If not given full and proper consideration, the cat itself will take over—as this story shows.

The Chi-Yen family had a wonderful cat. Because Mr. Chi-Yen held the cat in such high regard, he thought to call it "Tiger."

A neighbor remarked: "The Tiger is indeed a ferocious creature but he is hardly as mystical or cosmic as the Dragon. Cats are mystical and cosmic. You should change his name to 'Dragon.'"

Another neighbor saw the cat and said, "Without doubt the Dragon is more mystical than the Tiger. When it's flying in the upper air it takes its rest on a Cloud. This surely means

that a Cloud is mightier than the Dragon. You should change his name to 'Cloud.' "

But the other neighbors disagreed. They were quick to add their insights on the true naming of Mr. Chi-Yen's cat. One said: "When the dark Clouds take over the sky, who scatters them? Why, the Wind! You should change the cat's name to 'Wind.' "

A second cut in: "Of course the Wind is powerful. But when a great windstorm arises, where do we seek shelter? Behind the Walls of our houses! Walls hold back the fury of the Wind. Accordingly, you should change the cat's name to 'Wall.' "

"No, no, no," said another, "Of course, Walls are strong: No one is saying they are not. But not even the strongest Wall can withstand the gnawing tooth of the Rat. Surely the cat must be called 'Rat.' "

Mr. Chi-Yen, who had been listening patiently to all his neighbors, suddenly stood up when he heard this: "Of course! Now I understand why Cat is named 'Cat.' "

"I am sure that there are more than twenty different inflections in the language of cats, and their language is really a 'tongue,' for they always employ the same sound to express the same thing."

—FERNANDO GALIANI, BORN 1728,
PRIEST AND STATESMAN

WHY CAT AND DOG ALWAYS FIGHT

West African/Caribbean

"THE CAT AND DOG MAY KISS, YET ARE NONE THE BETTER FRIENDS."—PROVERB

A glance through these stories gives a hint of the great richness of African and Afro-Caribbean folklore. Of the vast repertoire of tales, the Anansi stories are justly famous, and strong candidates for inclusion. Unfortunately, I could choose only one, so I plumped for this amusing little tale with its vibrant personalities.

Anansi not know how Dog's mouth work. He call Dog "Friend Little Mouth." But when they eat together, Dog make just two swallows and all the food gone. Anansi think: "How this can be? Dog's mouth look small from outside, but him eat so quick."

One night come a big feast. Cat come. Dog come. But Cat and Dog do not eat at the same table. As Cat come up, Dog bare his teeth at her. Straightaway Anansi see exact way how Dog's mouth work, and him say to Dog: "Friend, I call you 'Friend Little Mouth,' but I wrong. I not know how your mouth work. But now I see when you lift your lips at Cat. I must thank Cat for this discovery. It was because of her that I find out the way it goes."

And that is the reason why today Cat and Dog never eat from the same plate: Dog bares his teeth at Cat because they are enemies.

" 'To begin with,' said the Cat, 'a dog's not mad. You grant that?'

" 'I suppose so,' said Alice.

" 'Well, then,' the Cat went on, 'you see a dog growls when its angry, and wags its tail when it's pleased. Now I growl when I'm pleased and wag my tail when I'm angry. Therefore I'm mad.' "

—FROM "THE CHESHIRE CAT,"
ALICE IN WONDERLAND
BY LEWIS CARROLL

THE CAT WHO WENT TO MECCA

Syrian

"WHEREVER MICE LAUGH AT A CAT, THERE IS A HOLE NEARBY."—PROVERB

Of all the stories here, this concise and beautifully structured little gem is one of my special favorites. Its wit and humanity, a feature of many Arabic folk tales, make it very appealing. With the newfound fervor of the pilgrim, this cat would agree with Oscar Wilde, that he can resist anything but temptation. (Of the flesh. Specifically, mouse.)

The king of the cats went on a pilgrimage to the holy city of Mecca. Upon his return, the king of the mice was obliged to pay him the traditional visit of congratulation on his safe return as a Hadji, or pilgrim.

He said to his mouse subjects, "Etiquette requires that we go to the house of the king of the cats and welcome him back formally." But his mice were alarmed at the prospect: "The cat is our mortal enemy. How can it be safe even to approach him?"

The king explained, "It's very simple! Now that he has been to Mecca and become a Hadji, the Holy Koran itself tells us that he is no longer free to do what was permitted beforehand. I hear he is very much a changed cat. He remains

at prayer from dawn to dusk, and I understand that the prayer beads never leave his paws the whole day. For such is the way of the Hadji, Allah be praised."

But the mice were not persuaded: "With respect, Your Majesty, perhaps it would be best if you were to call on him yourself, and see," they told the king of the mice. "We will wait here."

So the king of the mice set out to visit the new Hadji to welcome him back and to congratulate him. He poked his head out of the palace mousehole and surveyed the scene. There on the floor, not too far at all from the hole, kneeling on his own new prayer mat, was the king of the cats, wearing the white cap of a pilgrim on his head and deeply immersed in his prayers. He was loudly chanting and praising Allah. Every now and then he spit over his shoulder, first to his left side and then to his right, in order to drive off the ever-lurking devil who goeth about seeking to seduce us from our prayers.

But no sooner did cat see mouse peep out of his hole than the beads were dropped, the prayers were stopped, and—whoosh!—he sprang through the air. And but for Allah the Preserver, I can tell you he would have bitten that mouse's tail right off!

The king of the mice jumped back into his hole.

"How is the king of the cats after his pilgrimage?" the mice asked. "Has he indeed changed for the better?"

"We can forget about the pilgrimage," said the king of the mice. "Our friend may pray like a Hadji, but he still pounces like a cat!"

THE CAT
IN THE NIRVANA
PICTURE

Japanese

"THE CAT KNOWS WHOSE BEARD SHE
LICKS."—PROVERB

For all of its reputation of being the religion of compassion, Buddhism, apparently in common with almost all other religious persuasions, seems to suffer from certain ailurophobic tendencies—as this interesting legend reveals in passing.

The great Buddist artist Cho-Densu decided the time had come for him to paint his famous masterpiece, the Nirvana picture.

Each day a beautiful little smooth-haired cat came and sat quietly for him, and watched the progress of his painting.

Now the Nirvana picture showed the dying Buddha on a couch, surrounded by spirits, humans, animals, trees, and plants. This subject has been a favorite of Buddhist artists through the centuries.

The cat had noticed that, of all the animals, cats never appeared in Nirvana pictures. This saddened her, and she asked the great Cho-Densu why.

"That is a good question, little cat," said Cho-Densu, "and I will answer you. It is true that cats are not on the original list of animals protected by the Buddha. And it is also true

that the cat is never seen in a Nirvana picture. And the reason for this is that at the Buddha's funeral, there was, out of all the animals, one animal that fell asleep in the middle of the ceremony, and that animal, I am sorry to tell you, was the cat!"

The cat said nothing.

Now Cho-Densu was intensely involved in his painting. One day, he needed some ultramarine mineral for his coloring, but could find none. Wisely, he told the cat of his problem.

The next day not only did the cat bring the ultramarine mineral to Cho-Densu, but she also took him to the place where it could be found in abundance.

Cho-Densu was elated. To reward the cat, he decided to paint her into his Nirvana picture, and to this day she may still be seen in the enormous painting in the Tofukuji monastery in Kyoto.

"To gain the friendship of a cat is not an easy thing. It is a philosophic, well-regulated, tranquil animal, a creature of habit and a lover of order and cleanliness. It does not give its affections indiscriminately. It will consent to be your friend if you are worthy of the honor, but it will not be your slave."

—FROM "THE WHITE AND BLACK DYNASTIES" BY THEOPHILE GAUTIER

THE POT OF FAT

German

H ere, truly, is an engaging and, at the same time, a cynically twisted tale.

"Life," Jimmy Carter once remarked, "is not fair," and the truth of his own observation was further manifest for him in the 1980 election. The mouse in this story has a similar tale to tell.

One of the things that fascinated me about the stories that I have collected is the unerring degree to which each one mirrors the culture from which it comes. Some stories could be described as emotionally healthy, and—rather pointedly, I suggest—most of these seem to come from the poorer, so-called "third world" countries. Others come from the opposite end of the spectrum, and present realpolitik and cynicism as "the way of the world," as the cat, an advocate of the Big Lie, does in this story.

To sum up, by way of a simple moral, I present the following lines:

> When Puss professes Love of Mouse,
> Saying they should set up house
> When promised all this by a Cat
> A little Mouse should smell a Rat.

A cat met a mouse, and soon professed such love and affection for her that the mouse agreed they should live together.

"We must make provision for the winter," said the cat,

"or we will be hungry. And you, little mouse, must never stir out, or you will be caught in a trap."

So they bought a little pot of fat and hid it in the church, under the altar. "Nobody would steal it there," said the cat.

But, before long, the cat was possessed with a need for fat. All he could think about, all that day, was fat.

"Listen to me, little mouse," said he, "I have been asked by my cousin to stand godfather to a little son she has brought into the world; he is white with brown spots; the christening is today, so let me go, and you stay home and keep house."

"Oh yes, certainly," said the mouse, "go by all means. And when you are feasting, think of me; I should so like a drop of the sweet red wine."

But there was not a word of truth in all this. There was no cousin and no kitten. Instead, the cat went to the church and straight up to the altar, to the little pot, and licked the fat right off the top there and then, just like that!

Then he took a walk over the roofs of the town. He met up with his old cronies lying about. He stretched himself in the sun and yawned and licked his whiskers every time he thought of the pot of fat. In the evening he went home.

"There you are at last," said the mouse. "I expect you have had a merry time."

"Oh, pretty good, pretty good," said the cat.

"And what name did you give the child?" asked the mouse.

"Top-off," answered the cat after a slight pause.

"Top-off!" cried the mouse. "What a strange and wonderful name! Is it common in your family?"

"What does it matter?" said the cat. "It's not any worse than Krumpicker, like your godchild."

Well, soon the cat was again seized with a longing for fat.

"Guess what!" he said to the mouse. "Another christening, and they want me as godfather again; cute little fellow with a white ring around his neck. I could hardly refuse."

Of course the kind little mouse kept house, and the cat crept along the town wall until he reached the church, and going straight to the pot of fat, he proceeded to devour half of it.

Later the mouse asked what name had been given to the child.

"Half-gone," said the cat.

"Half-gone!" cried the mouse. "I never heard of such a name! I bet it's not to be found in the Saints' Calendar of Names."

Wouldn't you know but the cat soon was hankering after some more fat. He spoke to the mouse: "Good things always come in threes. Again I have been asked to be godfather; the little one is quite black with white feet, and not a white hair on its whole body, rare indeed! Of course, I have to go!"

"Top-off? Half-gone?" remarked the mouse. "Such curious names. I cannot but wonder at them!"

"That's because you always sit at home," said the cat, "never seeing the world, and fancying all sorts of things."

That day, the cat finished off the pot of fat, and spent the rest of the sunny afternoon sleeping it off on the roof of the church with a bunch of his reprobate pigeon-chasing pals.

Later the mouse inquired as to the name of the new child.

"Oh, I don't suppose it will please you any more than the others. It was named 'All-gone.'"

"All-gone?" cried the mouse, musing half to herself. "I never met anything like it! All-gone? Whatever can it mean?"

(After that the cat was not again asked to be godfather.)

Now of course, eventually winter came and—it becoming ever harder to find food—the mouse began to think of the pot under the altar. One day she said, "Cat, are you thinking what I'm thinking?"

"What?" asked the cat.

"Fat! Let's fetch our pot of fat today. Oh, how good it will taste, to be sure!"

"Indeed it will," said that cat, "just as good as if you stuck your tongue out the window!"

So they set out, and when they reached the hiding place they found the pot, but—to Mouse's horror—it was empty! Suddenly it came to her: "Oh, now I see it all. Some god-father! I didn't know they use grease for christenings! Top-off, indeed! Half-gone!—"

"Hold your tongue!" said the cat ominously. "One more word out of you and you'll be in grease yourself!"

But it was too late. "All-gone" was on Mouse's tongue; out it came, and the cat leaped on her and made an end of her.

And that is the way of the world.

"Lat take a cat, and fostre him wel with milk,
And tendre flesh, and make his couche of silk,
And lat him seen a mous go by the wal;
Anon he weyveth milk, and flesh, and al,
And every deyntee that is in that hous,
Swich appetyt hath he to ete a mous."

—FROM *THE MANCIPLE'S TALE*,
BY GEOFFREY CHAUCER

THE CAT AND
THE SERPENT

American Indian

"THE CAT DID IT."—PROVERB

There exists, of course, an enormous and very rich repository of American Indian folk tales. Unfortunately, very few of them are about cats, for the simple reason that cats apparently arrived in America with the white man. So I was pleased to find this charming little tale, even if the cat in question is a bit too far over on the kinder and gentler end of the feline spectrum!

Long, long ago, when animals could talk and spirits dwelled in the forest, a beautiful boy was born. When his mother looked in his eyes she knew he was no mere mortal: "The gods have sent us one of their own."

He was a strong but gentle boy, full of compassion, and when he grew up, he was called the Magician.

But a great plague came upon the people, and the Magician knew that he had to leave to search in the forest for the silver-leafed plant, the only antidote.

In the forest reigned Irmah the Serpent, and from its abode no one had ever returned. The Magician's dog asked to come with him, to protect him, but was told: "It is too dangerous."

But a little cat followed the Magician secretly, and when they were deep in the forest she jumped onto the Magician's

shoulder, saying: "Dear Master, I love you; when others spurned me, you were kind. Now I will protect you from the Serpent."

The Magician thanked her, but smiled at the idea of one so small protecting him. But for all his wisdom, he had not yet learned that the weak of the world are often chosen to confound the mighty.

That night as he slept, from deep in the forest the great Serpent crept nearer and nearer and coiled its body, ready to strike the Magician. But the cat attacked the huge snake and engaged it in a death struggle. With her swift and sure movements and sharp claws and teeth, again and again she wounded it, and again and again avoided its fangs, until finally she overcame the Great Serpent just at sunrise. The Magician awoke to find the monster dead and the forest freed from evil.

"Little cat, little cat," said the Magician, "what can I do to show my gratitude? What can I give you to repay you?"

To which the cat replied: "I desire that I no longer be an outcast. Let me enter the wigwams and be a friend of the people. Let me share the fireside of the lonely."

And it was given to her.

"He possessed nothing in the world except a cat, which he carried in his bosom, frequently caressing it, as his sole companion."

—JACOBUS DIACONUS, SAID OF
ST. GREGORY THE GREAT, WHO
RETIRED TO A MONASTERY AND
DIED IN A.D. 604

WHY GOATS CANNOT CLIMB TREES

Haitian/Caribbean

"IF YOU HAVE NO TROUBLE, BUY A GOAT." — PROVERB

As we know, it is the loose lips that sink ships, and this careless loose-lipped Goat came perilously close to altering the course of history. The balance of power 'twixt Cat and Dog could also have been shifted, with Goat passing on to Dog certain tree-climbing methodologies developed by Cat.

One day Goat see Cat climbing tree, him say to Cat, "How you do that?"

Cat say, "Easy. You put one foot like this, and another foot like that, and another foot like this, and the other foot like that."

And Goat, who was slow in the head, say, "One foot like what?"

And Cat say, "Come back to this tree tomorrow and I show you some more."

And Goat come back a second day, and Cat show him some more how to climb tree.

And again, Goat come back the third day, and Cat show him some more how to climb tree.

And on the fourth day, when Cat was coming to the tree

to teach Goat, she see Goat trying to teach Dog what Cat teach him: "One foot like that, another foot like this, and so forth." Lucky that Goat got it all backwards.

But Cat, she furious with Goat all the same: "Mister Know-it-all! Don't you know that Dog chases Cat, and Cat's only trick is to climb Tree. How do you presume to give my secret to Dog?"

Goat opened his mouth, but only silence come out!

"Well, Mister Goat, for that you will stay on the ground." And from that day to this, Cat keep her secret.

And that is why today Goat cannot climb a tree. Because him not pay attention to Cat's lesson, him only know how to stand on his back legs and nibble on low branches.

THE COURT
OF THE CATS

Irish

**"IT'S FOR HER OWN GOOD THAT
THE CAT PURRS."—PROVERB**

Here is another famous cat tale from Ireland dealing with the mysterious powers of cats, a moral fantasy that would make an Alfred Hitchcock or an Edgar Allan Poe envious. A farmer punishes a ginger tom for stealing food, and gets his comeuppance that very night when his case comes up . . . in the Court of the Cats!

Well now, this is a famous case that happened in the County of Clare some years ago. There was this farmer and every night he'd cook up a feed of swede turnips, beets, and mangolds for his cows, in one of those big old heavy cast-iron pots with the heavy lids. But the queer thing was, every morning he'd come down to find the lid moved over and a fair bit of his mash gone.

Well, he wasn't standing for that, was he, so he hides behind the kitchen dresser one night, and faith, in creeps this ginger tom, up to the pot, shifts the lid and helps himself. The farmer ups and gives him a fierce welt with his stick.

Well, the cat takes off with a yelp, and the farmer, pleased with the solving of the mystery and the punishment of the culprit, heads for bed. But, and here's the thing of it, no sooner was he in bed, but the bedroom door creaks open and

in files a long line of cats, maybe a dozen or so, and the ginger tom last, still hobbling from the welting he got from the farmer, and they sit in a court circle.

And in comes a big black tom, all business, and from atop a stool, calls the court to order—the judge, you see. And they argue the farmer's guilt or just cause back and forth most of the night, with all the airs of powder-wig barristers at the assizes. And now and then they'd stop, turn, and stare at the farmer, and him shaking with fright in his bed.

And then His Lordship, the black tom, holds up a paw for silence. And he deliberates a long while with brows knitted, and his lips pursed, rocking back and forth. And suddenly he stands up and says, "Not guilty!"

Well, the cats file out, and your farmer falls in a faint with relief. For I tell you, it's many the man today is walking around without the sight of his eyes, scratched out after losing his case in the court of the cats!

"Black Minnaloushe stared at the moon,
For, wander and wail as he would,
The pure cold light in the sky
Troubled his animal blood."

—FROM "THE CAT AND THE MOON"
BY W. B. YEATS

TIBB'S CAT
AND THE
APPLETREE MAN

English

**"THE CAT WHO COULD NOT REACH THE
SAUSAGE SAYS, 'I'M FASTING: TODAY IS
FRIDAY.' "—PROVERB**

*This English tale from Somerset, with its quirky humor,
is surely an antecedent, if several generations removed,
of the splendid Monty Python. Somerset, in the southwest of
England, was, incidentally, a powerful Celtic center of old, which
explains why a reference to the gathering of cats on the Celtic
festival nights would be made here.*

Down at Old Tibb's Orchards, in Zomerzet,
where the zider apples grows, were a cat who were proper
curious, 'er were.

And down past the orchards, with their rows 'n rows of
zider apple trees were a dark and marshy field, with elder
trees growin', and a low moaning sort of wind, like the sound
of voices just too far to make out what them are saying. A
gloomy, insidious sort of field, and no one in their right mind
went there, except them wild black cats as gathered there on
witchy nights, Belthane, Candlemas, and All 'allowes Eve.

Well, Old Tibb's cat were so curious she fixed on visitin'
the gloomy field. And as 'er were makin' 'er way through the

orchards, the Appletree Man called out to 'er: "Yew go on back to your 'ome, little cat. The gloomy field bain't no place for the likes of yew. There's folk comin' to put zider in my roots, and beat slapsticks to frighten off the witches. So off 'ome with yew, my dear, and don't yew ever come 'ere again until Saint Tibbs Eve."

Well, the little cat were proper frightened, 'er were, and she shot out of the orchard with her tail stock straight and stiffer 'n a poker. Proper frightened 'er, did the Appletree Man.

And she never wandered down by the gloomy field again because she didn't know when Saint Tibb's Eve was. Nor does anyone else!

CHIMNEY CORNER

African

"NO ONE TEACHES A CAT TO LOOK INTO A CALABASH."—PROVERB

I don't know the comparative IQs of cats and dogs, and I'm not sure if the zoologist-behaviorists have ever put them to the test, but certainly all folklore is very clear on which is the smarter animal: Cats win by a whisker, and a tail—and then some! And this story from Africa just makes the case all over again.

With Rain Season soon coming, Man wanted build house for himself. Him collect all material, then ask Dog to help him. But Dog say him busy with many, many things to do: run around, bark, hunt, chase, sleep in shade, scratch, yawn, catch fleas, wag tail.

"Too much dog business to do," say Dog, "no time for building houses."

So then Man ask Cat to help him build house. Cat say she busy with many, many things to do: sleep, yawn, wash, wait by mousehole, catch mouse, growl at bird, lie down, jump up, mee-ow, and rub her tail against everything.

"Very much Cat business to do," say Cat. But Cat, who is always a home lover, say, "But all that can wait until tomorrow. I will help you build your house."

And when the house was all built, Man say to Cat:

"Come in by the fire, Cat, and take your place in the chimney corner."

But him say to Dog he would have to sleep outside under the moon and stars.

And that is how Cat and Dog got their sleep places.

"He blinks upon the hearth-rug
And yawns in deep content,
Accepting all the comforts
That Providence has sent."

—FROM "ON A CAT AGING"
BY ALEXANDER GRAY

THE TALE
OF THE
PERSIAN CAT

Persian

"THAT CAT IS OUT OF KIND THAT SWEET MILK WILL NOT LAP."—PROVERB

The opening of this lovely little tale bears a certain resemblance to the famous parable of the Good Samaritan in its style, its setting, and its universal humanity. A merchant goes out of his way to help a stranger, who later reveals his true identity and repays the merchant in a magical way.

A certain merchant of Isfahan, arriving by caravan late at night at an oasis, came upon a group of brigands in the act of beating and robbing a stranger.

Having dispersed the ruffians into the desert, the merchant turned to help the unfortunate stranger into the caravansary, paid for his bed and food, and insisted on staying with him until he recovered.

The next evening, the stranger—praise be to the Great One—was sufficiently restored to be able to sit with the merchant by a fire outside the tent. High above the dark green palm trees, the stars shone bright and crisp in the midnight blue of the sky. The smoke from the fire coiled gently upwards in a cooling breeze, forming and reforming itself into an endless procession of shifting shapes.

After a long silence in which they both gazed into the fire, the stranger touched the merchant on the sleeve and said: "My friend, you knew nothing about me, but you did not hesitate to come to my rescue, with no expectation of recompense, which is a true mark of a great soul.

"But now I wish to give you a gift in return. You did not know that I am a magician, and can give you anything in the world that you desire."

The merchant replied: "I have lived a very good and happy life with my family. I have been successful in my trading, and right now could desire nothing more than to sit here in this beautiful and peaceful place, watching the fire, the swirling smoke, and the stars."

The magician nodded. "Very well. I shall therefore make for you a gift out of those very materials, so you shall have it forever." And he took a little tongue of fire, and the light of two distant stars, and a skein of swirling gray smoke, and kneaded and formed it in the basket of his deftly moving hands. And there came from within a sweet mewing sound and a rich purr, and out crept the most wonderful little cat that ever had been seen, with thick short gray fur, bright eyes, and fire-tipped tongue. And it played and purred, and waved its tail like the swirling smoke.

The magician bade the merchant: "Take this great soul back to your home, and it will be a friend to your family and a thing of beauty in your household for the rest of your days."

And that is the strange and wonderful story of how the Persian Cat came into this world.

THE CAT'S
BAPTISM

Haitian

**"A DOG'S PRAYER DOES NOT GO UP TO
HEAVEN."—PROVERB**

*If the reader doesn't quite understand the language of this
elaborate baptismal liturgy it is because it is in Cat Latin,
the language of all cat religious services before the sweeping
changes of Vaticat II. Students of cat church history will no doubt
be interested to note that, in those days, the congregation didn't
just hang out in pews: They got in there and actively participated
in the service. Parts of the ritual were even improvised!*

Little Kitten was due for baptism and Mr. and
Mrs. Cat picked her uncle on her second cousin's side to be
the godfather. They made the arrangements with the local
parish priest for the following Sunday at ten o'clock in the
baptistry. They invited all their relatives to the service and a
sit-down breakfast afterwards.

Sunday morning was gloriously sunny as the Cat family
and relatives walked to church in their very finest clothes.
The dignified party sat in the front rows of the bright little
wooden church, with Mrs. Cat holding Little Kitten wrapped
in a lace shawl. Father Felix and his two altar-cats entered
from the sacristy, and the venerable old priest climbed the
pulpit steps.

The baptismal service began as Father Felix intoned:

"Mee-ow, mee-ow, mee-ow,

mee-ow, mee-ow, mee-ow."

The entire congregation responded accordingly:

"Mee-ow, mee-ow, mee-ow,

mee-ow, mee-ow, mee-ow."

Father Felix turned the page of his missal, coughed, and continued:

"Mee-ow, mee-ow, mee-ow,

mee-ow, mee-ow, mee-ow."

The congregation responded:

"Mee-ow, mee-ow, mee-ow,

mee-ow, mee-ow, mee-ow."

Father Felix motioned with his hand for silence, and signaled for the godfather to step forward to the baptismal font with Little Kitten wrapped in her lace shawl. There was a silence. Father Felix motioned to him to begin the baptismal chant. The godfather cleared his throat and sang:

"Mee-ow."

"I'm sorry," said Father Felix, "I don't understand. What was that you just chanted?"

Again the godfather sang:

"Mee-ow?"

"No, no, no, no," said Father Felix, with a little exasperation, "it goes like this."

He intoned: "Mee-ow."

"That's what I just chanted," said the godfather.

Some of the other cats in the church were scandalized by the godfather's contradiction of Father Felix. One of them scampered across the altar and clipped the godfather on the side of his head with his paw.

"Yow! Yow!" said the godfather.

Two other cats chased after that cat and gave him a good scratching.

"Yow! Yow!" he said.

Three other cats from the back of the church rushed forward and bit Father Felix on the tail, mistaking him for the godfather.

"Yow! Yow!

Yow! Yow!"

The two altar-cats took on the three and bit them in their napes. They went:

"Yow! Yow! Yow!

Yow! Yow! Yow!"

Soon every cat in the church was joining in the free-for-all baptism, which finished off like this:

"Mee-ow, mee-ow, mee-ow.

Yow! Yow! Yow!

Mee-ow, mee-ow, mee-ow.

Yow! Mee-ow. Yow! Mee-ow.

Yow! Yow! Mee-ow, mee-ow.

Yow! MEE-OW! Yow!

Yow! MEE-OW! Yow!

Mee-ow! Mee-ow! Mee-ow!

Mee-ow! Mee-ow! Mee-ow!

Yow! Yow! Yow!

Yow! Yow! Yow!"

Finally, Father Felix closed the book, turned to the congregation and said:

"A-meeow!"

To which they all responded:

"A-meeow!"

MAELDUNE

Irish

"**IT IS BAD LUCK TO CROSS A STREAM
CARRYING A CAT IN YOUR ARMS.**"—**PROVERB**

This is another one of those mysterious Irish cat stories, but this time we find a strange, surrealistic setting and a haunting atmosphere. Maeldune's brother fails to heed a warning and a cat teaches him a lesson he would never forget—if only he could remember!

Maeldune, a powerfully built young man with a head of black curls and eyes of hazel green, was the adopted son of an Irish queen. One day he set out in a sailboat with his three foster brothers on an adventure.

After a long journey on a sea of glass, they arrived at an island shrouded in mist, in the middle of which stood a stout-walled fort, inside of which were several white-walled houses. Maeldune and his three foster brothers entered the largest of the houses, only to find within it a cat leaping and dancing by itself on the tiled floor between four pillars.

The cat paid them not the slightest heed as it went about its strange movements. The four young men saw a dazzling array of treasures hanging in rows on the walls beyond. The first row consisted of the most beautiful silver and gold brooches, made with the most extraordinary filigree workmanship. The next row was of exquisite silver and gold necklaces and torques, each one more wonderful than the next. And the last row was of swords fashioned with silver and gold hilts, again worked in the most intricate detail.

In the middle of the dining hall they beheld a great ox roasting on a spit, and on the thick oaken trestle table nearby, places set and gold and silver flagons of the finest wines.

Maeldune addressed the cat: "Kind Sir, may I inquire if this food and drink has been prepared for us?"

The cat interrupted its activity for the briefest of moments, stared coolly at him, and just as soon returned to its play. This Maeldune interpreted as an affirmative, and he and his foster brothers sat down at the oaken table and ate and drank their fill. And afterward, they slept.

In the morning, as they prepared to leave, Maeldune warned the three brothers not to take anything from the fort. But despite his warning, the youngest brother could not resist taking one of the brooches. They had not reached the door when the little cat leaped at the thief and went clean through him, like a fiery arrow shot from a longbow! The youngest brother was burned through and through, until all that was left was a pile of ashes on the flag floor.

Maeldune replaced on the wall the brooch that had been stolen, and then spoke softly to the cat, bidding it farewell. And scattering the ashes of the brother on the waters, they sailed for home.

"Cats, no less liquid than their shadows,
Offer no angles to the wind.
They slip, diminished, neat, through loopholes
Less than themselves."

—FROM "CATS"
BY A. S. J. TESSIMOND

THE TORMENT
OF
SAINT FRANCIS

Italian

**"WELL KENS THE MOUSE WHEN THE CAT'S
OUT OF THE HOUSE."—PROVERB**

This one is also a great favorite, a cosmic epic that tickles the soul with its great wit and fresh language. The Devil cannot abide Saint Francis's insufferable holiness, and so dispatches a fiendish horde of mice to Assisi to subvert his sanctity. A ghastly menu of temptations follow, but guess who comes to Francis's rescue?

It was God who created the cat, but the Devil made the mouse. Wasn't it a mouse that gnawed a hole in the Ark, and nearly drowned the whole of creation, if it hadn't been caught by the cat? And the frog that crept into the hole and puffed himself up and stopped the Ark from sinking?

Well, that's the way the mice are, and of course that's the way the Devil is, bad losers. Remember Saint Francis! Oh, the Devil hates holiness. The more he sees of it, the less he likes it. Most of his time is spent concentrating on attacking and undermining the really holy people. It's no fun for him seducing us poor mortals, who go about day to day trying to eek out a little solace with the odd venial infringement or two and, from time to time, an infraction of the holy code. That's all just so much bread and olive oil for Satan. Easy pickings. No, it's the saints that Satan goes after. They are the plums the Devil loves to pick, the plums that he daydreams of picking.

The more the Devil heard of Saint Francis the less he liked him, too. There was a saint so holy that the Devil took a week off from General Tormenting to plot and plan Francis's downfall.

"Let me think about this," said Old Scratch, stroking that greasy old beard of his.

And then it came to him: "Mice! Of course! Mice are an irritation, a distraction, a veritable thorn in the spiritual side. Let us visit one hundred handpicked mice on the good friar in his cell in that miserable monastery of his at Assisi, and let them divert him sufficiently from his prayers that he becomes weakened in grace for lack of spiritual nourishment, and in this weakened condition fall prey to a subsequent series of my most enticing material and illusory blandishments."

The more the Devil thought of the plan, the more he liked it. He went personally to the mouse caves and picked out one hundred mice of the order Mus Musculus, trained in the arts of spiritual subversion and demoralization. After exhorting them as befitted their special mission, they were duly dispatched to Assisi, where they took up residence in Francis's cell, and set about the infernal plan of eroding the saint's beatific equanimity, nibbling under his sandaled toenails, gnawing at the food on his plate *as* he attempted to eat it, and using his bed as a trampoline all night, from vespers till matins, so that within the week the frazzled Francis was the worse for wear from irritation, hunger, and sleeplessness.

But, my friends, God is not mocked; and whatsoever a mouse soweth, that shall he also reap, whether he be a harvest mouse or no. And, of course, it was not long before God heard of Francis's plight from the Exterminating Angel who likes to keep an eye on mice in his spare time. A countervailing plan was hatched in heaven, a mission for a mouser, a commission for a cat. A special tom, Felix, was picked out, briefed, exhorted, and dispatched to Francis, with whom he shared the plan.

The stage was set. The next night in the cell, some of the diabolic rodents, who knew their prayers backwards, but alas not forwards, had just started their infernal chorus to confuse poor Francis's vespers; others tugged out strands of his beard for nesting material; while yet others gnawed through his rosary and sent the hard beads bouncing across the flagstones of the cell floor where they would lie in wait to torment the bare feet of the unhinging monk as he groped about in the dark night of his soul, without so much as a candle.

The saint sat at his table, one arm resting on the surface, while the mice continued their onslaught. Suddenly, from out of the copious sleeve of the monk's brown habit shot our Felix, mowing down mice at every step, pouncing and darting, swiping and squeezing, clawing and clutching until out of the entire rodent rabble only two saved their miserable lives by reaching cracks in the walls of Francis's cell.

That is why today all the descendants of that heaven-sent cat will spend hours waiting by a crack in a wall. They want to finish the job so they can report back to headquarters!

THE PIOUS CAT

Omani

"HE WHO LIVES WITH CATS WILL GET A
TASTE FOR MICE."—PROVERB

The cat in this story would no doubt do very well today as a television evangelist—As I was early informed by my spiritual mentors, the devil cites scripture for his own purpose, and the cat here gets his "Blessing of the Rodents" mixed up with "Prayers before Meals", a perfectly understandable error, in the circumstances. But all's well that ends well, and it is nice to see the hypocrites lose one every now and again.

A cat sat warming himself by a brazier of charcoals that had been left out in the courtyard to be fanned by the breeze. Above his head a rat was creeping along the roof tiles. Seeing him, the cat suddenly called out, "Ya Haffeed! O Allah our Protector, preserve him!"

"Allah preserve nothing!" snapped back the rat. "What is this sudden interest in my well-being? Am I so special to you all at once?"

But just then the rat tripped over a waterspout and fell to the ground. In a flash the cat was upon him, and had caught him firmly in his claws.

"So, my little friend! When I called on Allah the Protector, you became blasphemous and said 'Allah preserve nothing!' Now you see the swift and terrible retribution that Allah the Merciful has wreaked on you for your irreverent scoffing!"

"Ah, how right you are, my dear fellow!" said the suddenly contrite rat. "I beg you, please don't kill me until I have a chance to atone; let me recite the Fatiha one last time before I die! In fact, I have an even better idea: Why don't you pray with me, and let us both say, 'May the Merciful One bring this affair to a just conclusion!' "

Impatient to get to his unexpected meal, the cat agreed. But, as he raised his paws in the attitude of prayer, the rat quickly escaped and ran to the safety of his hole.

So, tricked, the cat was left to wipe his eyes in sadness.

And that, my friends, is why today, whenever you see a cat put his paws to his face, you know he is remembering the smell of the rat that escaped that day, so long ago, in the courtyard.

Me and Pangur Bawn, my cat
Each has his aspiration.
Pangur's mind is set on mice
And mine on education.

More than any fame, I love
My books, pursuing learning;
Nor does my friend envy me—
Mice are Pangur's yearning.

—FROM "PANGUR BAWN,"
9TH-CENTURY OLD IRISH,
TRANSLATION BY MALACHI McCORMICK

THE MICE
OF SCHILDBURG

German

"SINGED CATS LIVE LONG."—PROVERB

*his extraordinary folk chronicle caricatures the passion,
stupidity, and cruelty of the mob, and can hardly fail to
suggest resonances of the Germany of the thirties. Especially
powerful is the image of a town disappearing without trace,
history, or record.*

*I suspect that I am not the first to make this observation.
Nonetheless, I was struck, in the course of my research, by a sense
of dark cloud that moves through many of the German folk tales.
(It is present, too, in the other German tale here, "The Pot of
Fat.") It seems not too outlandish to suggest that a centuries-old
body of folk tales that deal in violence, might-is-right, and a
strong and often cruel authority, might be a factor in program-
ming and predisposing a nation through its children. In a more
modern respect, it might make us wonder again at the long-term
effects of our own television diet (the new folklore).*

One day, a long time ago, a strange young man
wearing a multicolored cloak and carrying a cat in his arms
walked into the town square of Schildburg.

Now, there were no cats in the town of Schildburg, and
the local citizens, who had never seen a cat, gathered round
the young man and asked him what manner of beast it was.

"This beast is a mouser," he told them.

Well, the citizens may never have seen a cat, but they had seen too many mice. Mice were overrunning the town of Schildburg, and eating everyone out of house and home.

And granary. The floor of the town granary was a seething, moving brown and gray carpet of voracious mice, eating the grain so fast and frenzied that full sacks of wheat were emptying as quickly as pricked balloons before their very eyes.

"A mouser?" they said. "Will you sell it to us?"

"Yes," said the young man, and they settled there and then on a very high price.

Now in truth the young man did not know how good a mouser the cat was, and being concerned to keep the money he had just received, he decided to leave Schildburg quickly. As he was going out the town gate, the citizens asked for more information about the cat:

"What does it eat?"

"What you please," answered the young man over his shoulder.

Well, the citizens of Schildburg were all a little hard of hearing, and they misheard the young man, thinking he had said, "Men and beasts!" And some of the citizens thought that this sounded very dangerous, and they feared the cat.

That afternoon, it was decided to try out the cat in the town granary. But the citizens who feared the cat decided that they should kill it off.

"After it has eaten all the mice, it will eat all our pigs, and after it has eaten all our pigs, it will eat all our sheep, and after it has eaten all our sheep, it will eat all our cows, and after it has eaten all our cows, it will turn on us and eat us all up. So, we must kill it now."

But they were so afraid of the cat that they decided to burn down the granary with the cat inside it.

As soon as the cat smelled the smoke and saw the flames shooting high, it leaped out of a window and ran to a nearby house. The Schildburgers ran after it and set fire to that house too.

As the house was burning, the cat appeared on its roof and began to wash itself.

"Look," said the Schildburgers, "it is raising its paw to heaven and making the sign of vengeance."

Some of the citizens took a long pole and tried to strike the cat down. But it simply took hold of the pole and slid down it into the midst of the crowd, which immediately panicked and ran into the burgermeister's house. The cat made its escape in the confusion and ran away from Schildburg.

The flames spread so fast and the Schildburgers were so frightened that they all ran away. The rest of the houses in the town soon burned down, and finally the burgermeister's house burned down, and the chancery next door, which contained all the legal papers and guild lists and wills and historical documents and the town charter and property deeds and lists of inhabitants and genealogies and family bibles and census records. Everything was reduced to ashes.

And that is the reason why today the town of Schildburg does not appear on any map or in any history book or in the memory of any living person. The citizens were all so stupid and so afraid of one little cat that they allowed their whole town to burn down to the ground and disappear without trace, and never even attempted to put the fire out.

LITTLE KITTEN AND LITTLE RAT

African/Caribbean

"TO PUT THE CAT AMONG THE PIGEONS." — PROVERB

Like many of the Caribbean folk tales, this rather touching and sensitive story originated in Africa, where there are many versions of it still to be found today. In this one, the young friends, Little Kitten and Little Rat, have to grow up suddenly when their parents fill them in on a certain fact of adult cat and rat life.

Once upon a time Little Kitten and Little Rat were the closest of friends. They took turns chasing each other until they were so tired they fell down on the ground and then they would laugh together. And they would go exploring at the edge of the jungle, looking into things, and under things, and behind things, and creeping up on things, and pouncing on them, only to discover, as often as not, that it was the tip of the other's tail.

And then when they were tired, they would find a soft patch of sand or dried grass and curl up together to sleep. Then they would wake up and start all over again. And they were the best of friends.

One evening, when Little Rat got home after playing all day, Mother Rat asked her what she had been doing.

"Playing with my friend Little Kitten."

"You must not play with Little Kitten. Rats are what Cats most like to eat!"

The same evening, when Little Kitten got home after playing all day, Mother Cat asked her what she had been doing.

"Playing with my friend Little Rat."

"That doesn't make sense. Don't you know that Rats are for Cats to eat, not play with?"

The next day, Little Kitten and Little Rat met again. They looked at each other for a long time. Then each told the other what her mother had said. They agreed that they should not play together again. They were sad.

"I wish they hadn't told us," said Little Kitten.

"I wonder what would have happened if they hadn't told us," said Little Rat.

"Now we'll never know! Well, goodbye, my friend. I hope we never meet again."

"What in hell have I done to deserve all these kittens?"
—MEHITABEL IN "MEHITABEL HAS AN
      ADVENTURE" BY DON MARQUIS

JERJIS

Persian

Here is another Persian tale, representing another splendid chapter in the chronicles of the eternal war of cat against mouse. We learn of an unexpected property of the name of the prophet "Jerjis" (as opposed to, say, "Mohammed": The reader may wish to try pronouncing it for him/her self). Indeed, it is a difference that holds considerable fringe benefits for our fast-thinking Puss! The set-up is perfect and the punchline nothing short of masterful!

It was the cat's job to keep the mosque free of mice. Each day he was to be seen at the back of the mosque with his prayer mat spread out on the floor, kneeling and bowing down in prayer to the Merciful One.

But, whereas the eyes of the rest of the faithful at prayer were closed or directed toward Mecca, the eyes of the mosque cat were constantly sweeping the floors and the edges of the steps, and the entrance to the mosque, and especially the cracks and gaps in the beautiful tiled walls.

All vigilance is rewarded in the end, as the Prophet tells us. And so it was with the cat, who one day spied a sleek brown mouse creeping along the inside of the mosque wall.

"So, prayer really works!" remarked the cat to himself. "I must try this more often."

As he followed the mouse's progress, he absent-mindedly rolled up his prayer mat and put it away. He then crept stealthily to one of the enormous columns that held up the roof of the mosque and, having positioned himself next to the cul-de-sac where the column merged with the wall, lay in wait for his prey.

In due course, around the curve of the column scuttled the mouse, where, to his horror, he was confronted by the mosque cat, who promptly pounced on him and held him fast in his tightly clenched jaws.

Seeing his predicament, the mouse quickly realized that there was little time left to him in which to bargain for his life. His mind groped for inspiration.

"Before I depart this world," said the mouse to the cat, "please grant me one last, dying request. You who are so holy, I beseech you in the Name of Allah the Merciful, please do me the inestimable favor of pronouncing the Holy Name of one of the great Prophets—any one—so that it will be a sacred blessing on my soul on its journey into the hereafter."

The cat thought for a moment and then said simply, "Jerjis!" choosing the name of the one Prophet in the Holy Book that he could pronounce while keeping his jaws tightly clenched!

And that is why today Muslims will say of one who accedes to a request without losing the advantage, "Of all the prophets, you *would* choose Jerjis!"

FOOD FOR CATS

Jewish

"THE CAT SHUTS ITS EYES WHILE IT
STEALS CREAM."—PROVERB

*P*uss once again demonstrates her natural-born intelligence and her independent turn of mind in this famous old Jewish legend. The theme here is echoed by a number of stories, all of which hinge on what happens when inattentive scullery servant meets opportunistic cat!

At the beginning of the world, the Almighty called a meeting of all the newly created animals and asked each one where they would like to get their food from. Some said this, some said that, some said the other.

When it came to the cat, the Almighty asked her where she would like to get her food from.

"Do you want to get your food from the shopkeeper or from the fisherman or from the farmer?"

And the cat thought about each one in turn, and then replied:

"Thank you for offering me all these wonderful choices. But please, don't go to any trouble on my account. All I ask you to arrange is that the housewife forgets to close the kitchen door, and I will help myself!"

TOM TILDRUM

English

**"HE IS LIKE A CAT; FLING HIM
WHICH WAY YOU WILL, HE'LL LIGHT
ON HIS LEGS."—PROVERB**

I was fascinated to discover this English tale, which incorporates elements of two Irish stories here, "The Cat in Inchigeela Graveyard" and "The Court of the Cats." The outcome, however—in my opinion—is not as felicitous, because the teller seems to try too hard, but the similarities to the other stories make it worthwhile to read.

**O**ne cold and windy wintery evening, the sexton's wife was sitting by the fireside with her big black cat, Old Tom, both of them half asleep and waiting for the sexton to come home from the churchyard. Suddenly he burst in, saying, "Who's Tom Tildrum?" in such a wild way that both wife and cat stared at him to know what was the matter.

"Oh, I've had such a scare. I was digging away at Old Mr. Fordyce's grave when, well I suppose I must have dropped off, and woke up to a cat's Mee-ow. So I looked over the edge of the grave, and guess what I saw?"

"What?" said the sexton's wife.

"Why, nine black cats all like our friend Tom here, all with a white spot on their chests. And what do you think they were carrying? Why, a small coffin covered with a black velvet pall, and on the pall was a small gold coronet, and at every third step they cried all together, 'Mee-ow.'"

"And their eyes shone out with a ghostly green light, and they came toward me carrying the coffin, and the biggest cat of all walking in front."

"Go on, go on," said his wife.

"Well, as I was saying, they came toward me slowly and solemnly, and at every third step cried, 'Mee-ow.' "

"They stood right opposite Mr. Fordyce's grave, and looked straight at me. I felt right queer, I did! But look at Old Tom; he's looking at me the same way!"

"Go on, go on," said his wife, anxious for him to get on with the story, "never mind Old Tom."

"Where was I? Oh yes, they all looked at me, when the one not carrying the coffin came forward and, staring right at me, says to me, 'Tell Tom Tildrum that Tim Toldrum's dead!' "

"Look at Old Tom, look at Old Tom!" screamed his wife.

And well she might, for our cat was swelling up and staring, and shrieked out, "What! Old Tim dead! Then I'm the King of the Cats!" and he rushed up the chimney, and was never more seen.

"The [British Post Office] Cat System was inaugurated in the autumn of 1868, when the Money Order Office in London asked the Secretary of the Post Office for two shillings a week to feed three cats. The Secretary authorized their hiring, but refused to pay more than a shilling a week for the support of all three, saying 'They must depend on the mice for the remainder of their emoluments.' "

—FROM *THE CAT* BY MURIEL BEADLE

THE TALE
OF THE
MANX CAT

Manx

**"THE MORE YOU RUB A CAT ON THE RUMP, THE
HIGHER SHE SETS HER TAIL." — PROVERB**

*ere we have another tale connected with Noah's Ark, a
popular reference point for folk tales, apparently. In this
particular one, we are informed of certain events in and around
the aforementioned Ark, leading up to the disappearance of the
tail of the cat in question, the original Manx cat. This tailless-
ness, this absence, has of course hitherto been variously ascribed
to any number of causes, from Darwin's ideas of evolution to The
Devil. Here now it is revealed that it was, in reality, the door of
the Ark that did it!*

*By the way of historical footnote, it has long been claimed that
a wayward galleon of the Spanish Armada deposited several
tailless Moggies (a Cockney term of affection for a cat) on the
Isle of Man in 1588, there to breed in splendid isolation. The
claim is authoritatively disputed by well-known cat writer Muriel
Beadle, who points out that not only is tailless-ness not a particular feature of Spanish cats, but also, that such cats in the 1800s
in England were known as "Cornwall Cats." Ms. Beadle further
asserts that tailless cats, being much more common in the Orient,
were far more likely to be on board a bark from China, which
would be more likely to go aground off Cornwall!*

It is a controversy that I feel I should steer clear of, except perhaps to question if a bark could be considered a suitable mode of transport for a cat!

The tale of the Manx Cat is as old as the creation itself, very nearly, because it goes all the way back to Noah and his Ark.

By the end of the fourth page of the Bible, God was already fed up with man and said he would blot him out from the face of the earth and that he was sorry he had ever made him.

And God told Noah, who was the only good man left in a bad bunch, how to build a big Ark out of gopherwood and how many cubits and such, and put the door up high in the side, and take the animals and birds and creeping things on board the Ark, because He was sending a Great Flood that would wash away and drown anyone and anything that wasn't on the Ark.

And He said, by the way, the Flood starts at noon sharp next Tuesday, so be sure you're good and ready, and all packed, and don't—whatever you do—be late, because once the Flood starts, woe betide anyone who gets locked out of the Ark.

And Noah said not to worry, they'd all be there on time, and that he'd see to it.

So then Noah had a meeting of all the animals and gave them strict instructions on what to bring and under no circumstances were they to be late, because they'd find themselves locked out, and he didn't have to tell them what that meant.

And Puss said, "That only gives me a week to catch all the

mice." So she set out to catch the mice and by Tuesday morning she had most of them caught, and Dog said "Ah, come on, that's as near as dammit, get on the Ark so you can get a good place and keep your fur dry."

But Puss said no, she was going to finish the job. And off she went, pouncing on mice left, right, and center. And so intent was she on getting the job done that she hardly noticed the time going by, and the big drops of rain—as big as cups of water—that were beginning to fall. And the sky darkened, and thunder rolled in the heavens, and lightning split the skies, and Noah and his wife and Dog were at the door of the Ark shouting at Puss to hurry up, look at the time, and Puss saying hold on, there's just one more mouse left.

And she would have stayed out there, except that at the very stroke of twelve, the mouse ran through the door of the Ark, just as Noah and his wife and Dog were shutting the door, with God pushing from the outside, and Puss j-u-s-t managed to squeeze her body through the heavy closing door.

But not the tail, which fell off into the sea as the Ark sailed away.

And that is the tale of how the Manx cat lost its tail.

"This time, it vanished quite slowly, beginning with the end of the tail, and ending with the grin, which remained some time after the rest of it had gone."

—FROM "THE CHESHIRE CAT,"
ALICE IN WONDERLAND
BY LEWIS CARROLL

THE PUBLIC HOUSE CAT AND MOUSE

Irish

"ALE WILL MAKE A CAT SPEAK."—PROVERB

Has Cat ever chased Mouse with such unrelenting intent as does our Puss here from Limavady in County Derry? And has Mouse in a tight corner ever thought faster on his feet —or, should we say, in his bath?

In coming up with this story, I suspect that I may have unwittingly uncovered the true cultural heritage and original source of the Tom and Jerry cartoon! As we read of the chase we can hear those tire squeals. Now, if only the cartoons could emulate the elegant ending!

In the country of Ireland, in the county of Derry, in the town of Limavady (which means "the leap of the dog"), in the main bar, in Michael John MacDaid's pub, in the middle of the night, the pub cat was chasing the pub mouse.

Oh, what a chase it was! Across the floor, up on the bar, over the till, onto the shelves, along the bottles, beside the porter barrels, between the stools, beneath the dartboard, out the door, in the window, behind the yard brush, through the snug, past the statue of the Blessed Virgin Mary, by the photograph of President Kennedy, the photograph of Pope John Paul, the photograph of the Derry Hurling team, and the big jar of pennies for the African Orphans, down into the crates of Orange Squash, and left of the tray of washed pint glasses, where Michael John himself had left the soap out where he never left it before, only he had to go and fix the dartboard, which had split dangerously in the middle of the Limavady and District Dart Finals.

Michael John left the soap out where he had never left it before, and the mouse slipped on it, and somersaulted three times head over tail, and landed splash in an open barrel of porter!

"Ochone, ochone," said the mouse, drowning in the Black Sea, all his life flashing before him in his last minutes, a life of being chased endlessly by Puss the Cat over the same route, across the floor, up on the bar, over the till . . . and left of the tray of washed pint glasses, and down into his hole, only tonight, there was the soap left out where it had never been left out before; it was always in the soap dish. And now look!

Just then, Puss the Cat poked his head over the top of the barrel of porter.

"Well, will ye look!" said the cat, thinking himself very witty, because *luc* is the Irish word for mouse. Naturally, the mouse didn't appreciate the humor.

"Please! Please! Save me! Save me!" begged the mouse, gulping and spluttering porter and going down for the third time. "Get me out of here! Please!"

"What's your hurry?" asked the cat. "If I were to pull you out, it would only be to eat you. Now you know that, don't you?"

"I don't care, I don't care," said the desperate mouse, again gulping porter, and going down for the fourth time. "Please get me out of the barrel, and believe me, you can do whatever you want with me. It's the idea of drowning in a barrel of porter that I just can't abide!"

"Well, all right, since you put it that way," said the cat, reaching down into the barrel with its paw, pulling the mouse to safety, and placing it on the tea towel next to the tray of washed porter glasses.

But quicker than you could say "the leap of the dog," the mouse was off, running through the rows of porter glasses, and leaping off the edge of the tray, he disappeared down his hole in a flash, the hot steamy breath of his pursuer enveloping him like a fog. Puss the Cat was furious.

"Fair play, now! Fair play," he screamed. "Didn't you just give me your word down in that barrel of porter that if I pulled you out of the drink, you would let me eat you up?"

"Well, that's as may be," said the mouse, slowly scratching his head, "but tell me, didn't your mother ever tell you not to believe a word out of someone who has drink taken?"

"Ignorant people think it's the noise which fighting cats make that is so aggravating, but it ain't so: it's the sickening grammar they use."

—MARK TWAIN

THE DEVOUT CAT

Indian

"IF THE CAT HAD WINGS SHE'D CHOKE
ALL THE BIRDS IN THE AIR.''—PROVERB

One of the classic themes of cat folk tales is the disguise of feline intentions, the feigned, airy "who, me?" disinterest in a targeted prey. Another theme is the creation of the illusion that, yes, the cat in question has achieved the cat-equivalent of altered maculation in leopards. It may involve presenting oneself as a reformed pilgrim just back from Mecca, or, as in the case of this old Hindu tale, building up a reputation as a wise old judge who happens to be a little hard of hearing, thereby making it necessary for both parties in the proceedings (as it happens, a plump duck and a juicy hare) to come a little closer . . . .

A duck and a hare have a fierce argument over the ownership of a home.

"I was here first," said the duck adamantly, putting his webbed foot down.

"Why, that's ridiculous," said the hare, twitching his whiskers fiercely. "There *was* nothing here until I arrived!"

There was no resolving the argument.

"You'll just have to take it to the judge," said the others.

Now the judge is a sly old cat who has cultivated a favorable reputation by doing good acts. He is respected by the duck and the hare because they have heard that the cat fasts all day, prays all night, and would never harm the smallest

hair or feather on the head of any creature.

When the cat sees them approaching, he puts a saintly expression on his face and begins to recite a prayer from the Bhagavad-Gita. The duck and the hare approach him with great respect, apologizing for the intrusion of their worldly affairs on one so spiritual. The benign old cat puts them at ease, graciously dismissing their concern over the intrusion, and asks them to explain their problem to him.

The hare and the duck tell him both versions of the story. The cat listens sagely, nodding wisely from time to time, and interjecting a grave "Yes. Yes. I see." The duck and the hare notice that the cat is straining slightly, as if trying to catch their every word. At the end, he apologizes to them, saying he has missed a few of their points, and could they approach the bench, as it were, and speak into his ear, which they do.

As soon as they come near him, the old cat pounces on both the duck and the hare and eats them up.

"If a cat is creeping up on prey and realizes that another cat is watching, it will straighten up and act disinterested. When meeting on friendly or neutral ground, one cat will stop its approach if the other looks at it directly. In courtship, the female looks about casually; if she looked directly at her partner, it would stop the action. . . . When rival cats fight, however, they *do* look directly at each other."

—FROM "VERHALTENSSTUDIEN AN KATZEN" BY GERMAN ZOOLOGIST PAUL LEYHAUSEN

THE TALE
OF SISTER CAT

Italian

**"A CAT THAT LICKS THE SPIT IS NOT TO
BE TRUSTED WITH ROAST MEAT."—PROVERB**

When living in Rome some years ago, I came across several versions of this old Italian tale; no matter how they
varied in their lists of suitors and cycles of mourners, they all had
that fresh and exuberant Decameronic zest that makes for an
irresistible story. The reader will notice an initial similarity with
"The Pot of Fat" in the way in which cat and mouse get together,
but the story soon develops in a completely different way.

There once was a cat who was anxious to get
married. So she decided to buy some red and white makeup
to paint her face and make it beautiful. Having done that,
she went to an upstairs open window and sat and waited
there for a likely prospect to pass by.

After a while some cows passed by the house. Seeing the
cat in the window, one of the cows asked her, "What's the
matter, cat? What are you doing up there at the window?"

"Well," she said, "don't you know? I'm going to get married. I am going to find a husband." So the cow said, "Would
you like me for a husband?" And the cat said, "First, I must
hear your voice." And the cow went like this: "Moo-Moo!"
And the cat was so scared she almost jumped out of her skin.
She replied, "Get along with you! Your voice is terrible!"

Next came some goats, and one offered himself as husband. "Let me hear your voice," said the cat. The goat cleared his throat and went like this: "Meh-eh-hehheh, Meh-eh-hehheh!" and the cat said, "Oh, no! I'm sorry but you scare me. Go away! How did you ever get a voice like that?"

Next came some rats. One said, "Hello, Sister Cat, what are you doing up there?" "Well, don't you know I am a pretty girl and I'm going to get married? I'm looking for a husband." And the rat said, "So, how would you like to have me as a husband?" "First, let me hear your voice," said the cat. The rat went, "Squeak-squeak!" And the cat said, "Your voice scares me, I don't like it: It needs oiling. Go away!"

Next came a group of mice. The smallest one said to her, "Hello, Sister Cat, what are you doing up there at the window?" "Why, don't you know? I am a pretty girl and I am going to get married. I am looking for a husband." The little mouse said, "How about me?" "First let me hear your voice," said the cat. The little mouse went, "Squik, squik, squik!"

And the cat said, "Oh, little mouse, what a sweet little voice. Come upstairs: You suit me wonderfully well!"

So up the stairs went the little mouse. And they ate dinner, and all went well and all that, and then, the next morning, the cat said, "Now, my dear little mouse, since this is the Feast Day of Saint Francis, who is certainly our patron saint, you look after the soup while I go to Mass!"

But even the happiest households are not immune to tragedy. Sad to tell but the mouse got too close to the soup pot, lost his balance, fell in, and drowned. By the time the cat came back after Mass, the mouse was all cooked up, and the cat didn't know it. She started calling for him, "Brother Mouse! Brother Mouse!" She looked under the table and behind the door and under the bed, but to no avail! Finally she went to look in the pot, and found poor mouse's goose well cooked, so to speak!

She took him out and started crying, "Poor Brother Mouse!" And the window answered, "Why do you cry, Sister Cat?" "I cry because Brother Mouse is dead!" And the window started mourning and rattling loudly.

Then the door heard this and asked, "Window, why do you mourn?" "Don't you know? Brother Mouse is dead and the cat is crying and since I am a window, I rattle for mourning." And the door said, "And since I am a door, I'll open and close for mourning."

Then a tree heard and said, "Oh, door, why do you mourn?" And the door said, "Don't you know? Brother Mouse is dead; the cat is crying; the window is rattling; and since I am a door, I close and open all the time." And the tree said, "And since I am a tree, I shake off my leaves for mourning."

Then a dog went by and said, "Tree, why are you shaking off your leaves?" The tree said, "Because Brother Mouse is dead; the cat is crying; the window is rattling; the door is closing and opening; and since I am a tree, I shake off all my leaves." "And since I am a dog, I keep on running."

Then the fountain asked, "Dog, why do you run?" Dog said, "Oh, don't you know? Brother Mouse is dead; the cat is crying; the window is rattling; the door is opening and closing; the tree is shaking off all its leaves; and since I am a dog, I keep on running." And the fountain said, "And since I am a fountain, I won't give any water."

The servant of the King was passing by with her bucket and asked the fountain, "Fountain, why don't you have any

water?" "Oh," the fountain said, "don't you know? Brother Mouse is dead; the cat is crying; the window is rattling; the door is opening and closing; the tree is shaking off its leaves; the dog is running; and since I am the fountain, I don't give any water." And the servant said, "In which case, since I am the servant, I'll break my bucket."

Then the servant went to the Queen without water, and the Queen asked, "Why did you break the bucket?" "Well," the servant said, "don't you know? Brother Mouse is dead; the cat is crying; the window is rattling; the door is opening and closing; the tree is shaking off its leaves; the dog is running; the fountain isn't giving any water; and since I am the servant, I broke my bucket."

Then the queen said, "And since I am the Queen, I'll throw myself on the flour bag." So, in came the King and said, "Why, my dear, are you on the flour bag?" The Queen said, "Don't you know? Brother Mouse is dead; the cat is crying; the window is rattling; the door is opening and closing; the tree is shaking off its leaves; the dog is running; the fountain isn't giving any water; the servant broke her bucket; and since I am the Queen, I threw myself on the flour bag."

"Very well," said the King, "and since I am the King, I'll throw myself on the Queen!"

And this is why all psalms end up with "Gloria!"

"It's not only this we praise, it's the general love:
Let cat's mew rise to a scream on the tool-shed
roof."

—FROM "PROTHALAMION"
BY W. H. AUDEN

WHY PEOPLE
HAVE
ONLY ONE LIFE

African / Caribbean

"A CAT HAS NINE LIVES."—PROVERB

his is another one of my special favorites in the collection. Again, Cat wins the IQ contest with Dog (actually, it's no contest). The conversation at the end between cat and a surprisingly casual God is quite inspired. The Deity, incidentally, seems to favor that "detached management style" which has been in such vogue recently.

One day, Cat and Dog were talking.

Cat said: "Man is born. He lives. He dies. And when he dies, he doesn't live again."

And Dog said: "That's not true. Yes, Man is born. He lives. He dies. But when he dies he is born again, and lives, and dies again."

And so they argued. But neither one could persuade the other.

And then Cat said: "In the morning we will go to ask God how it is."

And Dog said: "Good idea, let us go." But immediately he began to put a plan into action which would ensure that he got to God first: He placed along the way to heaven little pieces of fat of the sort that he knew Cat was especially fond

of. "Cat will stop to eat the pieces of fat along the way, and so I shall arrive before her."

But Cat also had a plan to delay Dog: "Let me put out bones along the way, so that when Dog sees them he won't be able to resist stopping and chewing on them. And you know how long Dog spends chewing on even one bone." So she placed the bones along the way.

In the morning they set out on their journey. First they came to where Dog had put out some fat for Cat. And Dog said to himself, "Now watch Cat make a pig of herself." But Cat did not stop.

Then they came to where Cat had put out one of her bones for Dog, and Dog said to himself: "What a stroke of luck! Now I won't be hungry on the journey." And he stopped to gnaw on the bone, while Cat continued on.

And of course, each time she came to some fat, Cat was not deterred. But each time Dog came to a bone, he stopped to gnaw on it. And so he fell farther and farther behind, and Cat soon arrived at God's house in heaven.

Straightaway she asked God the question: "When Man dies, does he rise again, or when he dies, is that it?"

And God said: "What an interesting question. I never thought about it. What do you think?"

And Cat told God that she believed that when man died, that was it. He didn't rise again.

And God replied: "Then that's the way it will be!"

And when Dog finally arrived at God's house and asked his question, God told him how the question had been settled earlier with Cat.

And so it came to be that just for the sake of a few bones, Man knows only one journey on this earth.